DK WORKBOOKS

3rd Grade

Cursive Writing

Author Brenda Apsley
Consultant Linda Ruggieri

DK London
Editors Elizabeth Blakemore, Jolyon Goddard
US Editor Margaret Parrish
Managing Editor Christine Stroyan
Managing Art Editor Anna Hall
Senior Production Editor Andy Hilliard
Senior Production Controller Jude Crozier
Jacket Design Development Manager Sophia MTT
Publisher Andrew Macintyre
Associate Publishing Director Liz Wheeler
Art Director Karen Self
Publishing Director Jonathan Metcalf

DK Delhi
Project Editor Neha Ruth Samuel
Editor Nandini Gupta
Art Editors Rashika Kachroo, Baibhav Parida
Managing Editors Soma B. Chowdhury, Kingshuk Ghoshal
Managing Art Editors Ahlawat Gunjan, Govind Mittal
Senior DTP Designer Tarun Sharma
DTP Designers Anita Yadav, Rakesh Kumar, Harish Aggarwal
Senior Jacket Designer Suhita Dharamjit
Jackets Editorial Coordinator Priyanka Sharma

This American Edition, 2020
First American Edition, 2016
Published in the United States by DK Publishing
1450 Broadway, Suite 801, New York, NY 10018

A catalog record for this book is available from the Library of Congress.
ISBN: 978-1-4654-4470-7

DK books are available at special discounts when purchased in bulk
for sales promotions, premiums, fund-raising, or educational use.
For details, contact: DK Publishing Special Markets,
1450 Broadway, Suite 801, New York, NY 10018
SpecialSales@dk.com

Printed and bound in Canada

All images © Dorling Kindersley Limited
For further information see: www.dkimages.com

For the curious

www.dk.com

Contents

This chart lists all the topics in the book.
Once you have completed each page,
color a star in the correct box below.

FACTS

The lowercase alphabet is all the small letters we use to make words.

Follow the numbered arrows for direction and copy the letters of the alphabet in lowercase.

a   b   c   d   e   f   g

h   i   j   k   l   m   n

o   p   q   r   s   t   u

v   w   x   y   z

FACTS

Ascenders are parts of letters that go above the body of the letter. Descenders are parts of letters that go below the body of the letter.

Copy the letters below, which have ascenders. Fill the lines.

b

h

Copy the letters below, which have descenders. Fill the lines.

g

p

z

Copy the letter *f* below, which has both an ascender and a descender. Fill the line.

f

★ More Lowercase Practice

The lowercase letters *i* and *j* have a dot. The lowercase letter *t* has a bar, which is the line that goes across the letter.

Copy the letters below. For each letter, add the dot or bar last of all. Fill the lines. **Note:** *t* also has an ascender and *j* also has a descender.

i

j

t

Now practice writing the lowercase letters that don't have ascenders, descenders, dots, or bars. Fill the lines.

a

c

u

x

FACTS

Most letters join to the next letter with a line curving up from the baseline to the top of the body of the next letter, for example, *am*, *are*, and *us*.

Practice writing these words in cursive handwriting.

us	....	*an*	....
am	....	*use*	....
arm	....	*free*	....
can	....	*new*	....
may	....	*came*	....
hand	....	*man*	....
name	....	*happy*	....

Use the words in the box to label the picture.

face	arm	hand	head

FACTS

The letters *h, o, v,* and *w* join to most letters with a line above the baseline that curves up to the top of the next letter, for example, *be, on, van,* and *we.*

Copy these words in cursive handwriting.

on	....	*be*	....
boy	....	*bee*	....
win	....	*we*	....
our	....	*was*	....
big	....	*oven*	....
voice	....	*very*	....
wood	....	*brown*	....

Use the words in the box to label the pictures.

boy	wasps	van	orange

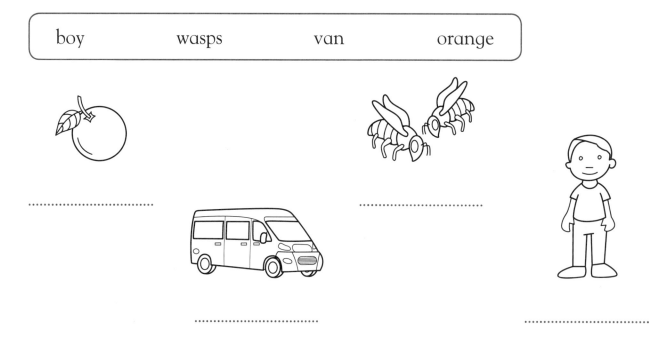

....

....

FACTS

Most letters join to letters with ascenders with a line that goes from the baseline up to the top of the ascender of the next letter, for example, **all**, **it**, and **elf**.

Practice writing these words in cursive handwriting.

it	....	*at*	....
all	....	*the*	....
elf	....	*full*	....
with	....	*help*	....
want	....	*crab*	....
little	....	*calf*	....
about	....	*pull*	....
school	....	*should*	....

Use the words in the box to label the picture.

rabbit	plants	water

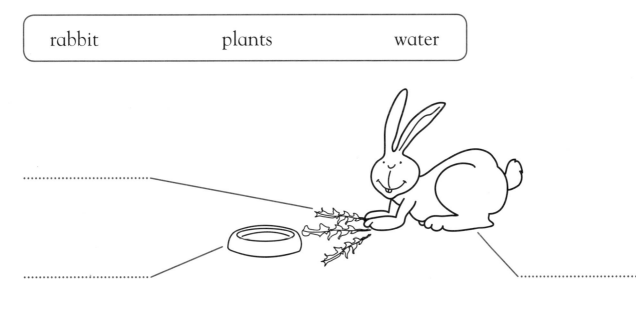

FACTS

The letters *h*, *o*, and *w* join to letters with ascenders with a line above the baseline that curves up to the top of the ascender of the next letter, for example, *bl*, *oh*, and *wh*. In English words, the letter *v* is not followed by a letter with an ascender.

Practice writing these words in cursive handwriting.

old	....	of	....	owl	....
hawk	....	oboe	....	book	....
look	....	not	....	who	....
blue	....	why	....	when	....
what	....	holly	....	where	....

Use the words in the box to label the pictures.

owl	book	strawberry	bowl

....

....

Copy the words below in cursive handwriting.

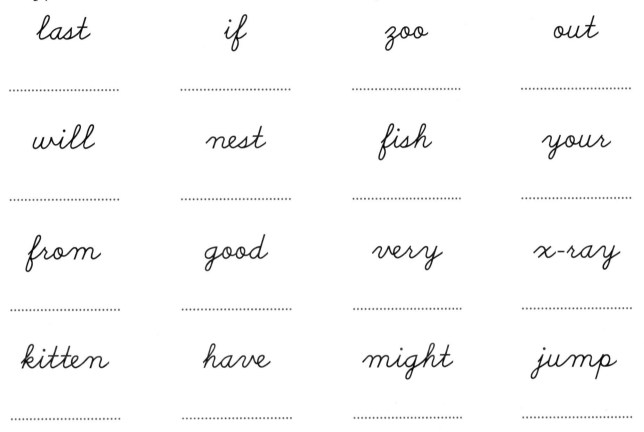

last   if   zoo   out

will   nest   fish   your

from   good   very   x-ray

kitten   have   might   jump

Write labels for the pictures below in cursive handwriting.

Copy these words, which all contain letters with ascenders, descenders, or both.

for ....

zip ....

quiet ....

guide ....

quiz ....

useful ....

fifteen ....

packed ....

joyful ....

laughter ....

Follow the strings from the balloons and write labels for the pictures inside.

....

Pangrams ⭐

A pangram is a sentence that includes all 26 letters of the alphabet.

The sentences below are pangrams. Copy these in your best cursive handwriting.

The quick brown fox jumps over the lazy dog.

....

....

The zebra, jay, fox, pig, and my wolves quack!

....

....

Pack my red box with five dozen quality jugs!

....

....

Make up another pangram. Prepare it on scrap paper first. You can use some of the words given in the box. See if you can write a pangram that makes sense!

| zip | pizza | kite | exit | x-ray | banjo | key | quit |

....

....

....

....

Uppercase letters are also called capital letters. New sentences and proper nouns begin with uppercase letters.

Follow the numbered arrows for direction and copy the uppercase letters.

The uppercase letters $\mathcal{D}$, $\mathcal{O}$, P, $\mathcal{V}$, and $\mathcal{W}$ do not join to the next letter at the beginning of words. All the other uppercase letters join to the next letter. **Note:** $\mathcal{Y}$ and $\mathcal{Z}$ have descenders and $\mathcal{F}$ has a bar.

Copy the following proper nouns in your neatest cursive handwriting.

Zurich	....	Utah	....
Logan	....	Spain	....
Xavier	....	Alaska	....
Yukon	....	Brazil	....
Russia	....	George	....
Hawaii	....	India	....
Thomas	....	Quebec	....
Florida	....	Nevada	....
England	....	Maryland	....
California	....	Kentucky	....

Now copy these words. They all begin with an uppercase letter that does not join to the next letter.

Ohio	....	Paul	....
Velma	....	Oliver	....
William	....	David	....
Virginia	....	Panama	....

FACTS

Names are proper nouns. They begin with an uppercase letter.

Below are some names of children. Make one list of the boys' names and another of the girls' names. Write the names on the lists in alphabetical order.

Zack	Flora	Peter	Katy
Harry	Vanessa	Rob	Lily

Boys

....

....

....

....

Girls

....

....

....

....

Label these pictures whose names start with an *s*. Use cursive handwriting. Now number the words from 1 to 6 in alphabetical order.

The letters in these words are mixed up. Look at the pictures, then write the letters in the correct order to make words. Use cursive handwriting.

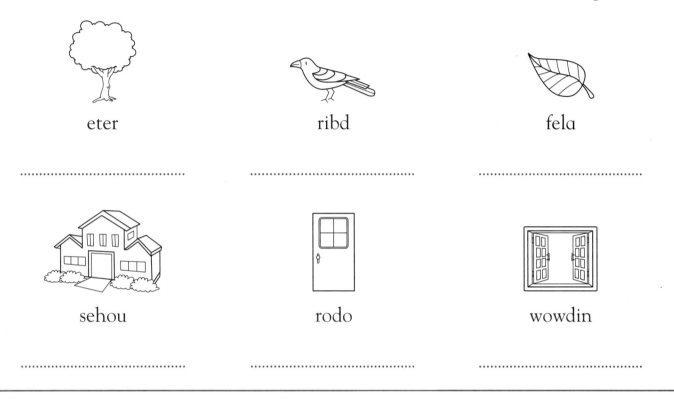

eter

ribd

fela

....

....

....

sehou

rodo

wowdin

....

....

....

Write each group of words in the correct order as sentences. Use your neatest cursive handwriting. **Remember:** The first word of a sentence needs an uppercase letter, and a sentence ends with either a period, a question mark, or an exclamation point.

eggs nest bird's there in are the three

....

what play shall we

....

play let's of game soccer a

....

★ | Numbers and Numerals

Read the numerals and number words. Then write the number words in your neatest cursive handwriting. **Remember:** Numerals are the symbols we use for numbers.

0 zero	....	10 ten	....
20 twenty	....	30 thirty	....
40 forty	....	50 fifty	....
60 sixty	....	70 seventy	....
80 eighty	....	90 ninety	....
	100 one hundred	....	

Write a number word to match each numeral. For number words above twenty, use hyphens (-) to join the tens and the units. For example, "21" is written as "twenty-one."

54 ....   23 ....

19 ....   31 ....

100 ....   70 ....

88 ....   62 ....

Write the number of your house or apartment and the number of children in your class in both numerals and number words.

Numeral   **Number Word**

....

....

Your letters should be the same size and shape unless they are uppercase letters. Leave the same amount of space between each word.

Copy this story neatly in your best cursive handwriting.

A Mouse's Idea

A big, fierce cat was very good at catching mice, so the mice always needed to know where she was. One young mouse had an idea. He said that if the mice put a bell around the cat's neck, it would ring when she moved. Then, they could run away. A wise old mouse agreed, but he had a question. Was there a mouse brave enough to tie the bell around the cat's neck?

Write the sentences below in cursive handwriting, using the correct punctuation marks from the box. **Remember:** Use uppercase letters at the beginning of sentences and proper nouns.

apostrophe '	comma ,	period .	question mark ?
	exclamation point !	"quotation marks"	

tom sara dan and lily are writing

....

what is your topic asked tom

....

its a surprise said sara

....

guess said dan loudly

....

Lily said its going to be about pets

....

A synonym is a word that has the same or a similar meaning as another word. For example, "large" can mean the same as "big."

Write some synonyms for these words in cursive handwriting.

vacation ....

nice ....

cold ....

like ....

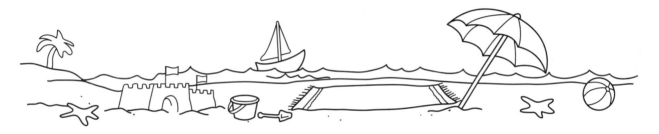

Imagine you are on vacation. Write a message to your class on the postcard below in cursive handwriting. Use some of the synonyms above and draw a stamp. **Remember:** Write your class name or number and the name and address of your school under the stamp.

Read the poem and think of a title for it. Write the title and the poem in your neatest cursive handwriting.

Way down south where bananas grow,
A grasshopper stepped on an elephant's toe.
The elephant said, with tears in his eyes,
"Pick on somebody your own size!"

....

....

....

....

....

Plenty of practice will improve your handwriting.

Copy this passage in your neatest cursive handwriting.

Whales live in the ocean. They look like very large fish, but they are mammals. They swim by moving their tails up and down, unlike fish, which move their tails from side to side. Like humans and other mammals, whales need air, so they have to swim up to the surface of the water to breathe. The blue whale is the largest animal.

Days and months are proper nouns and start with uppercase letters.

Copy these sentences in your neatest cursive handwriting.

The seven days of the week are Sunday, Monday, Tuesday, Wednesday, Thursday, Friday, and Saturday.

....

....

....

....

The twelve months of the year are January, February, March, April, May, June, July, August, September, October, November, and December.

....

....

....

....

....

....

FACTS

Punctuation marks include periods, commas, question marks, exclamation points, apostrophes, and quotation marks. You can write two words in a shorter way, called a contraction, by using an apostrophe. For example, "we will" can also be written as "we'll."

Write the sentences below using lowercase and uppercase letters. Use the correct punctuation marks.

blue killer white gray and sperm are types of whales

....

....

which is the largest whale asked mr brown

....

....

i know mr brown said joe it is the blue whale

....

....

Using cursive handwriting, write these words in full and then as a contraction with an apostrophe. One has been done for you.

I will _I will_ _I'll_

do not ....

could not ....

would not ....

★ Planning a Story

FACTS

Paragraphs split up different parts of a story, making it easier to read and understand. Always start each paragraph on a new line.

Make a plan for a made-up, or fictitious, story. Write notes about something that is not real. It could be something you imagine, a toy or place, or an animal. **Remember:** You do not have to write notes in full sentences.

Plan the theme or the idea behind the story. For example, it could be a dream.

....

....

....

Plan the type of story. For example, it could be a mystery or an adventure.

....

....

Plan the time. For example, the story could be in the present, past, or future.

....

Plan the place. For example, the story could be set on Mars or at school.

....

Plan two characters and decide what they are like. For example, they could be silly or brave.

....

....

Write your story using the notes you made on the opposite page. Write the title and the author's name—that's you! Then draw a picture. Write in neat cursive handwriting. You'll probably need to finish your story on extra pieces of paper.

Title: ....

By: ....

....

....

....

....

....

....

....

....

....

....

Write this funny poem in your best cursive handwriting.
Remember: Write the title of the poem first.

The Young Lady of Niger

There was a young lady of Niger
Who smiled as she rode on a tiger.
They returned from the ride
With the lady inside,
And a smile on the face of the tiger!

....

....

....

....

....

Write about the poem. Say if you like it or not, and give your reasons.

....

....

....

Copy this passage in your neatest cursive handwriting.

Rain forests are very large, dense forests that grow where the weather is always wet and hot. The largest area of rain forest is in Brazil, in South America, around the Amazon River. The trees and other plants in a rain forest grow well because there is plenty of sunlight and water. About thirty million kinds of plants and animals live in these huge areas of forest.

★ Proofreading Your Work

Checking written work carefully is called proofreading. It helps you spot any mistakes you might have made.

Read the clue, proofread these sentences, and then write them correctly.

Clue: Write things that happen today in the present tense. For example, "I go to school." Write things that have already happened in the past tense. For example, "I went to school."

I hope we can played after school.

....

I go swimming last week.

....

I am seven years old last year.

....

Read the clue, proofread these sentences, and then write them correctly.

Clue: Write singular words for one of something, for example, "one bird." Write plural words for more than one, for example, "two birds."

There are a lot of cookie in the jar.

....

Look! Here comes a swarm of bee!

....

How many book is on the shelf?

....

Copy the start of this Greek myth in your neatest cursive handwriting.

Long ago, in Greece, there lived a boy named Icarus. He was sent to live on a faraway island with his father. They wanted to escape, but they did not have a boat, so they decided to fly away, like birds. They made two sets of wings using feathers, wax, and string. Then they tied the wings to their backs and flapped them, faster and faster, until they rose up into the air. They were flying!

....

....

....

....

....

....

....

....

....

Write the sentences below in cursive handwriting. Write each sentence twice, then put a check (✓) against the one you think is neater. **Remember:** Use punctuation marks and put uppercase letters in the correct places.

i wonder when the rain will stop

....

....

james turned when I called his name

....

....

wow what a great sports car

....

....

Now write four sentences of your own using words from the box.

| uncle | rain | goes | train |

....

....

....

....

Write this passage in your neatest cursive handwriting.

Dolphins are part of the same animal family as whales. They live in oceans and rivers in groups called pods. They are very smart animals and seem to like being with people. Dolphins make different noises as they play and feed together. These noises are their way of talking to each other.

Read this passage carefully. Check for mistakes and underline any errors you find. Rewrite the passage in your neatest cursive handwriting. Use correct spellings, uppercase and lowercase letters, and punctuation marks. **Hint:** The passage contains 24 errors.

kenneth grahame

kenneth grahame was born in scotland in 1859 he had a sun whose name was alastair but he call his son mouse he told his son stories about animals that lived by a riverbank he wrote the stories down in a book the title of the book is the wind in the willows

....

....

....

....

....

....

Copy this passage in your neatest cursive handwriting. It is from a book called *The Wind in the Willows*, written by Kenneth Grahame.

The Mole had been working very hard all the morning, spring-cleaning his little home. First with brooms, then with dusters; then on ladders and steps and chairs, with a brush and a pail of whitewash; till he had dust in his throat and eyes, and splashes of whitewash all over his black fur, and an aching back and weary arms.

FACTS

Nonfiction writing is about facts—things that are true.

Make a plan for a piece of nonfiction writing by answering the questions below. It can be about something that happened at school or information about a science topic, for example. Before writing the full piece on the opposite page, make brief notes to help you.

What is the piece of writing about?

....

....

What is the title of your piece?

....

What kind of nonfiction is it? For example, is it about an event in your life or in history, or a description of an animal?

....

....

Are there people in the piece? ....

Where or when does it take place? ....

What interesting details will you include in your piece?
For example, will you include conversations in it?

....

....

What happens in the end? ....

....

Begin by writing the title of the nonfiction piece and the author's name—that's your name! Write it in your best cursive handwriting, using the plan and notes you made on the opposite page.

Remember: Use paragraphs in your piece.

by ....

Write the sentences below in cursive handwriting. Write each sentence twice, then put a check (✓) against the one you think is neater. **Remember:** Use punctuation marks and put uppercase letters in the correct places.

do you like my new watch

....

....

will you show me how to skip please

....

....

lets go swimming tomorrow

....

....

Now write four sentences of your own using words from the box.

coin	without	know	young

....

....

....

....

Copy this short passage about the Amazon River in cursive handwriting. Write as neatly as you can.

The Amazon River in South America is the second-longest river in the world. It flows from mountains called the Andes for almost 4,000 miles into the Atlantic Ocean on the coast of Brazil. For most of its length, the river flows through areas of very thick tropical forest called rain forest, the home of a wide variety of plant and animal life.

★ Planning a Letter

Imagine that someone has sent you a very special birthday gift—a new computer! Plan a thank-you letter. **Remember:** Write short, quick notes. They do not need to be written neatly.

Write these words as labels on the letter plan below.

- Your name and address
- Love from ....
- Your signature
- Your message
- Dear .... ,
- The date

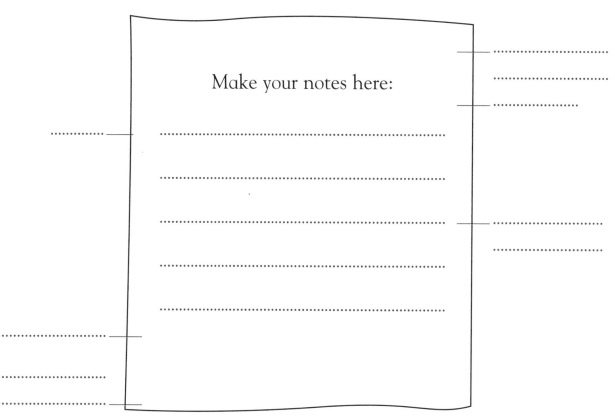

Make your notes here:

Write the person's name and address on the envelope. Draw a stamp. **Remember:** Write the zip code if you know it.

Look at the plan and notes you made on the opposite page before writing your thank-you letter. Write in your neatest cursive handwriting.
Remember: Write your address, the date, and the name of the person you are writing to. Sign your name at the end.

★ Favorite Things

FACTS

Proper nouns and the main words in titles all start with uppercase letters.

Write your favorite thing for each of the topics listed below.
Write in your neatest cursive handwriting.

color ....

movie ....

food ....

book ....

sport ....

animal ....

music group ....

TV program ....

Now write the name of your best friend in cursive handwriting. Then draw a picture of him or her.

....

....

Copy this passage in your neatest cursive handwriting.
It is from *The Jungle Book*, by Rudyard Kipling.

It was seven o'clock of a very warm evening in the Seeonee Hills when Father Wolf woke up from his day's rest, scratched himself, yawned, and spread out his paws one after the other to get rid of the sleepy feeling in their tips. Mother Wolf lay with her big gray nose dropped across her four tumbling, squealing cubs, and the moon shone into the mouth of the cave where they all lived.

....

....

....

....

....

....

....

....

Planning a Book Review

Fiction writing is about people and things that are made up or not real.

Make a plan for a book review of a book you have read.
Answer the questions below and write brief notes about the book.

What is the name of the book and the author?

....

What is the book about?

....

....

Who are the main characters in the book? **Remember:** Characters are the people in the book.

....

....

What are the events in the book? **Remember:** Events are the things that happen in the book.

....

....

What is your opinion of the book? Give reasons for liking or disliking it.
Remember: Your opinion is what you think of the book.

....

....

Write the book review in your best cursive handwriting using the plan and notes you made on the opposite page. **Remember:** Give a title to your book review and use paragraphs to make it easier to read and understand.

Copy this poem in your neatest cursive handwriting.

Clouds

White sheep, white sheep,
On a blue hill,
When the wind stops
You all stand still.
When the wind blows
You walk away slow.
White sheep, white sheep,
Where do you go?

Christina Rossetti

....

....

....

....

....

....

....

....

....

Fill in your personal profile in your best cursive handwriting.
Sign your name, then write the date at the bottom.

PERSONAL PROFILE

○ Name ....

○ Age ....

○ Date of birth ....

○ Address ....

....

....

○ Zip code ....

○ Parents ....

○ Brothers ....

○ Sisters ....

○ Best friends ....

○ Pets ....

○ Signature ....

○ Date ....

Certificate

3rd Grade

Congratulations to

....

for successfully finishing this book.

GOOD JOB!

You're a star.

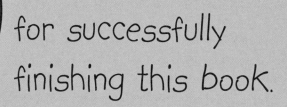

Date

....

Answer Section with Parents' Notes

This book is intended to introduce cursive handwriting skills to your child. The content features English language arts activities appropriate to third grade. Working through the activities will help your child to develop a neat style of cursive handwriting with regular letter formation and size.

Contents

The activities are intended to be completed by a child with adult support. In this book your child will practice:

- writing the lowercase alphabet;
- writing the uppercase alphabet;
- writing letters with ascenders and descenders;
- the different ways of joining cursive letters;
- writing words and number words;
- using casing and punctuation;
- copying poems and passages;
- planning and writing letters, book reviews, and stories;
- planning and writing nonfiction pieces.

How to Help Your Child

As you work through the pages with your child, make sure he or she understands what each activity requires. Read the facts, if present, and instructions aloud. Encourage questions and reinforce observations that will build confidence and increase active participation in classes at school.

The cursive font used in this book is based on the Zaner-Bloser style of handwriting. If your child has already learned cursive handwriting at school, he or she should continue to use that style in the activities even if it differs from the style of the letters and ways of joining letters outlined in this book.

Encourage your child to write slowly and neatly. Point out any mistakes your child makes or any incorrect letter formations and correct any spelling errors. In addition to making corrections, it is very important to praise your child's efforts and achievements. Good luck, and remember to have fun!

4

★ The Lowercase Alphabet

FACTS The lowercase alphabet is all the small letters we use to make words.

Follow the numbered arrows for direction and copy the letters of the alphabet in lowercase.

a b c d e f g
a b c d e f g
h i j k l m n
h i j k l m n
o p q r s t u
o p q r s t u
v w x y z
v w x y z

Explain that learning cursive handwriting will help your child to write entire words without lifting the pen or pencil from the paper. With practice, cursive writing goes faster than printing.

5

Ascenders and Descenders ★

FACTS Ascenders are parts of letters that go above the body of the letter. Descenders are parts of letters that go below the body of the letter.

Copy the letters below, which have ascenders. Fill the lines.

b b b b b b
h h h h h h

Copy the letters below, which have descenders. Fill the lines.

g g g g g g
p p p p p p
z z z z z

Copy the letter f below, which has both an ascender and a descender. Fill the line.

f f f f f f

Explain the terms "ascender" and "descender" to your child. You could also provide a separate piece of lined paper for your child to practice other letters with ascenders and descenders, such as d, k, l, q, and y, not covered on this page.

6

★ More Lowercase Practice

FACTS The lowercase letters i and j have a dot. The lowercase letter t has a bar, which is the line that goes across the letter.

Copy the letters below. For each letter, add the dot or bar last of all. Fill the lines. **Note:** t also has an ascender and j also has a descender.

i i i i i i
j j j j j j
t t t t t t

Now practice writing the lowercase letters that don't have ascenders, descenders, dots, or bars. Fill the lines.

a a a a a a
c c c c c c
w w w w w w
x x x x x x

The activities on this page will help your child understand that some lowercase letters are written with a dot or a bar (i, j, and t). You could also provide a separate piece of lined paper for your child to practice other letters without ascenders and descenders, such as e, m, n, o, r, s, u, and v, not covered on this page.

7

Joining Cursive Letters 1 ★

FACTS Most letters join to the next letter with a line curving up from the baseline to the top of the body of the next letter, for example, am, are, and us.

Practice writing these words in cursive handwriting.

us	us	an	an
am	am	use	use
arm	arm	free	free
can	can	new	new
may	may	came	came
hand	hand	man	man
name	name	happy	happy

Use the words in the box to label the picture.

| face | arm | hand | head |

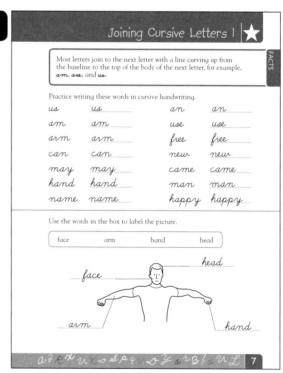

Practice will help your child write the cursive letters both correctly and consistently. Check the handwriting for consistency in the size and proportions of letters.

FACTS

The letters *b*, *o*, *v*, and *w* join to most letters with a line above the baseline that curves up to the top of the next letter, for example, *be*, *on*, *van*, and *we*.

Copy these words in cursive handwriting.

on	on	be	be
boy	boy	bee	bee
win	win	we	we
our	our	was	was
big	big	oven	oven
voice	voice	very	very
wood	wood	brown	brown

Use the words in the box to label the pictures.

boy	wasps	van	orange

orange

wasps

van

boy

8 *azxnkospqvoysrbfaul*

When writing, your child should sit comfortably, not too close to the writing surface, and hold a pen in a controlled, comfortable, but not too tight grip. It will help improve handwriting.

FACTS

Most letters join to letters with ascenders with a line that goes from the baseline up to the top of the ascender of the next letter, for example, *all*, *it*, and *elf*.

Practice writing these words in cursive handwriting.

it	it	at	at
all	all	the	the
elf	elf	full	full
with	with	help	help
want	want	crab	crab
little	little	calf	calf
about	about	pull	pull
school	school	should	should

Use the words in the box to label the picture.

rabbit	plants	water

plants

water

rabbit

azxnkospqvoysrbfaul 9

Handwriting, reading, and spelling are very closely linked to one another. Your child's progress in one skill will benefit the others.

FACTS

The letters *b*, *o*, and *w* join to letters with ascenders with a line above the baseline that curves up to the top of the ascender of the next letter, for example, *bl*, *oh*, and *wh*. In English words, the letter *v* is not followed by a letter with an ascender.

Practice writing these words in cursive handwriting.

old	old	of	of	owl	owl
hawk	hawk	oboe	oboe	book	book
look	look	not	not	who	who
blue	blue	why	why	when	when
what	what	holly	holly	where	where

Use the words in the box to label the pictures.

owl	book	strawberry	bowl

book

owl

bowl

strawberry

10 *azxnkospqvoysrbfaul*

Short but regular practice sessions in cursive handwriting will help your child develop a fluent, fast, legible, and confident style.

Copy the words below in cursive handwriting.

last	if	zoo	out
last	if	zoo	out
will	nest	fish	your
will	nest	fish	your
from	good	very	x-ray
from	good	very	x-ray
kitten	have	might	jump
kitten	have	might	jump

Write labels for the pictures below in cursive handwriting.

tree   pen   cloud   door   soap

ball   queen   cow   egg   ant

azxnkospqvoysrbfaul 11

Ensure that your child copies the words on this page correctly. It's best for the child to say the label for each picture first and then write it neatly. Remind your child to add dots and bars to words, if needed, after finishing writing the entire word.

12

★ More Ascenders and Descenders

Copy these words, which all contain letters with ascenders, descenders, or both.

for	for	for	for
zip	zip	zip	zip
quiet	quiet	quiet	quiet
guide	guide	guide	guide
quiz	quiz	quiz	quiz
useful	useful	useful	useful
fifteen	fifteen	fifteen	fifteen
packed	packed	packed	packed
joyful	joyful	joyful	joyful
laughter	laughter	laughter	laughter

Follow the strings from the balloons and write labels for the pictures inside.

jam   ball   fork   three

You can extend the exercise on this page by giving your child more words to write that contain letters with ascenders and descenders.

13

Pangrams ★

A pangram is a sentence that includes all 26 letters of the alphabet.

The sentences below are pangrams. Copy these in your best cursive handwriting.

The quick brown fox jumps over the lazy dog.

The quick brown fox jumps over the lazy dog.

The zebra, jay, fox, pig, and my wolves quack!

The zebra, jay, fox, pig, and my wolves quack!

Pack my red box with five dozen quality jugs!

Pack my red box with five dozen quality jugs!

Make up another pangram. Prepare it on scrap paper first. You can use some of the words given in the box. See if you can write a pangram that makes sense!

| zip | pizza | kite | exit | x-ray | banjo | key | quit |

Answers may vary

Provide scrap paper so that your child can plan the pangram. Help your child if necessary. Writing the letters of the alphabet and crossing them out as they are used will be helpful for this activity.

14

★ The Uppercase Alphabet

Uppercase letters are also called capital letters. New sentences and proper nouns begin with uppercase letters.

Follow the numbered arrows for direction and copy the uppercase letters.

A B C D E F G

A B C D E F G

H I J K L M N

H I J K L M N

O P Q R S T U

O P Q R S T U

V W X Y Z

V W X Y Z

Check your child's handwriting for neat, regular letter formation and size. Point out any features that need extra practice in a positive way, offering encouragement rather than criticism.

Using Uppercase Letters ★

The uppercase letters D, O, P, V, and W do not join to the next letter at the beginning of words. All the other uppercase letters join to the next letter. Note: Y and Z have descenders and T has a bar.

Copy the following proper nouns in your neatest cursive handwriting.

Zurich	Zurich	Utah	Utah
Logan	Logan	Spain	Spain
Xavier	Xavier	Alaska	Alaska
Yukon	Yukon	Brazil	Brazil
Russia	Russia	George	George
Hawaii	Hawaii	India	India
Thomas	Thomas	Quebec	Quebec
Florida	Florida	Nevada	Nevada
England	England	Maryland	Maryland
California	California	Kentucky	Kentucky

Now copy these words. They all begin with an uppercase letter that does not join to the next letter.

Ohio	Ohio	Paul	Paul
Velma	Velma	Oliver	Oliver
William	William	David	David
Virginia	Virginia	Panama	Panama

Explain that some uppercase letters do not join to the following letter. Your child should first read the names carefully and then begin copying them. Extend this activity by asking your child to make a list of the cities in your state.

★ Alphabetical Order

FACTS Names are proper nouns. They begin with an uppercase letter.

Below are some names of children. Make one list of the boys' names and another of the girls' names. Write the names on the lists in alphabetical order.

| Zack | Flora | | Peter | | Katy | |
| | Harry | Vanessa | | Rob | | Lily |

Boys
Harry
Peter
Rob
Zack

Girls
Flora
Katy
Lily
Vanessa

Label these pictures whose names start with an *s*. Use cursive handwriting. Now number the words from 1 to 6 in alphabetical order.

sack   1   spoon   4   shell   2

sun   6   star   5   sock   3

The names on this page should be written alphabetically and start with uppercase letters, which may or may not join the following letters. Your child should also understand how to arrange words alphabetically by looking at the second letters.

Ordering Letters and Words ★

The letters in these words are mixed up. Look at the pictures, then write the letters in the correct order to make words. Use cursive handwriting.

eter   ribd   fela
tree   bird   leaf

sehou   rodo   wowdin
house   door   window

Write each group of words in the correct order as sentences. Use your neatest cursive handwriting. **Remember:** The first word of a sentence needs an uppercase letter, and a sentence ends with either a period, a question mark, or an exclamation point.

eggs nest bird's there in are the three
There are three eggs in the bird's nest.

what play shall we
What shall we play?

play let's of game soccer a
Let's play a game of soccer!

Provide your child with scrap paper for figuring out the order of the letters in the first activity. In the second activity, check that the words are spelled correctly and that the reordered sentences start with uppercase letters and end with the correct punctuation mark.

★ Numbers and Numerals

Read the numerals and number words. Then write the number words in your neatest cursive handwriting. **Remember:** Numerals are the symbols we use for numbers.

0	zero	zero	10	ten	ten
20	twenty	twenty	30	thirty	thirty
40	forty	forty	50	fifty	fifty
60	sixty	sixty	70	seventy	seventy
80	eighty	eighty	90	ninety	ninety
100	one hundred	one hundred			

Write a number word to match each numeral. For number words above twenty, use hyphens (-) to join the tens and the units. For example, "21" is written as "twenty-one."

54	fifty-four	23	twenty-three
19	nineteen	31	thirty-one
100	one hundred	70	seventy
88	eighty-eight	62	sixty-two

Write the number of your house or apartment and the number of children in your class in both numerals and number words.

Numeral   **Number Word**

Answers may vary   Answers may vary

Explain the difference between numerals and number words. Make clear to your child that number words above twenty, such as "thirty-three" and "seventy-four," should always be written with a hyphen.

Handwriting Practice ★

FACTS Your letters should be the same size and shape unless they are uppercase letters. Leave the same amount of space between each word.

Copy this story neatly in your best cursive handwriting.

A Mouse's Idea

A big, fierce cat was very good at catching mice, so the mice always needed to know where she was. One young mouse had an idea. He said that if the mice put a bell around the cat's neck, it would ring when she moved. Then, they could run away. A wise old mouse agreed, but he had a question. Was there a mouse brave enough to tie the bell around the cat's neck?

A Mouse's Idea

A big, fierce cat was very good at catching mice, so the mice always needed to know where she was. One young mouse had an idea. He said that if the mice put a bell around the cat's neck, it would ring when she moved. Then, they could run away. A wise old mouse agreed, but he had a question. Was there a mouse brave enough to tie the bell around the cat's neck?

Give your child time for this practice piece, reading it through before copying it neatly and accurately using cursive handwriting. Also, ensure that there is equal spacing between the words.

20

★ Using Punctuation

Write the sentences below in cursive handwriting, using the correct punctuation marks from the box. **Remember:** Use uppercase letters at the beginning of sentences and proper nouns.

apostrophe '	comma ,	period .	question mark ?
exclamation point !		"quotation marks"	

tom sara dan and lily are writing

Tom, Sara, Dan, and Lily are writing.

what is your topic asked tom

"What is your topic?" asked Tom.

its a surprise said sara

"It's a surprise," said Sara.

guess said dan loudly

"Guess!" said Dan loudly.

Lily said its going to be about pets

Lily said, "It's going to be about pets."

Check your child's written work carefully to ensure that the spelling and punctuation are correct. Be ready to offer help, guidance, and encouragement.

21

Synonyms ★

A synonym is a word that has the same or a similar meaning as another word. For example, "large" can mean the same as "big."

Write some synonyms for these words in cursive handwriting.

vacation

nice

cold *Answers may vary*

like

Imagine you are on vacation. Write a message to your class on the postcard below in cursive handwriting. Use some of the synonyms above and draw a stamp. **Remember:** Write your class name or number and the name and address of your school under the stamp.

Answers may vary

Recognizing synonyms used in text and then thinking up and writing more of them will greatly improve your child's creative writing skills and vocabulary. If possible, demonstrate how a thesaurus can improve vocabulary.

22

★ A Poem

Read the poem and think of a title for it. Write the title and the poem in your neatest cursive handwriting.

Way down south where bananas grow,
A grasshopper stepped on an elephant's toe.
The elephant said, with tears in his eyes,
"Pick on somebody your own size!"

Answers may vary

Way down south where bananas grow,
A grasshopper stepped on an elephant's toe.
The elephant said, with tears in his eyes,
"Pick on somebody your own size!"

Confident readers will be able to read the poem on this page independently. Ensure that your child reads the poem loudly before copying it. Encourage careful writing. Make sure the poem has a title.

Handwriting Practice ★

Plenty of practice will improve your handwriting.

Copy this passage in your neatest cursive handwriting.

Whales live in the ocean. They look like very large fish, but they are mammals. They swim by moving their tails up and down, unlike fish, which move their tails from side to side. Like humans and other mammals, whales need air, so they have to swim up to the surface of the water to breathe. The blue whale is the largest animal.

Whales live in the ocean. They look like very large fish, but they are mammals. They swim by moving their tails up and down, unlike fish, which move their tails from side to side. Like humans and other mammals, whales need air, so they have to swim up to the surface of the water to breathe. The blue whale is the largest animal.

Encourage your child to read through the passage before copying it. That will familiarize your child with the topic. Check for neat and accurate letter formation.

★ Days and Months

FACTS

Days and months are proper nouns and start with uppercase letters.

Copy these sentences in your neatest cursive handwriting.

The seven days of the week are Sunday, Monday, Tuesday, Wednesday, Thursday, Friday, and Saturday.

The seven days of the week are Sunday, Monday, Tuesday, Wednesday, Thursday, Friday, and Saturday.

The twelve months of the year are January, February, March, April, May, June, July, August, September, October, November, and December.

The twelve months of the year are January, February, March, April, May, June, July, August, September, October, November, and December.

Remind your child about using uppercase letters in proper nouns. Check the answers for correct spellings and punctuation.

More Punctuation ★

FACTS

Punctuation marks include periods, commas, question marks, exclamation points, apostrophes, and quotation marks. You can write two words in a shorter way, called a contraction, by using an apostrophe. For example, "we will" can also be written as "we'll."

Write the sentences below using lowercase and uppercase letters. Use the correct punctuation marks.

blue killer white gray and sperm are types of whales

Blue, killer, white, gray, and sperm are types of whales.

which is the largest whale asked mr brown

"Which is the largest whale?" asked Mr. Brown.

i know mr brown said joe it is the blue whale

"I know, Mr. Brown," said Joe, "it is the blue whale."

Using cursive handwriting, write these words in full and then as a contraction with an apostrophe. One has been done for you.

I will	*I will*	*I'll*
do not	*do not*	*don't*
could not	*could not*	*couldn't*
would not	*would not*	*wouldn't*

Activities like these help to revise and reinforce the correct use of punctuation marks in your child's written work. You can also give your child extra examples of contractions, such as "can't," "she'll," and "didn't."

★ Planning a Story

FACTS

Paragraphs split up different parts of a story, making it easier to read and understand. Always start each paragraph on a new line.

Make a plan for a made-up, or fictitious, story. Write notes about something that is not real. It could be something you imagine, a toy or place, or an animal. **Remember:** You do not have to write notes in full sentences.

Plan the theme or the idea behind the story. For example, it could be a dream.

Answers may vary

Plan the type of story. For example, it could be a mystery or an adventure.

Answers may vary

Plan the time. For example, the story could be in the present, past, or future.

Answers may vary

Plan the place. For example, the story could be set on Mars or at school.

Answers may vary

Plan two characters and decide what they are like. For example, they could be silly or brave.

Answers may vary

Ensure that your child does not rush to begin the creative exercise. Explain how it's worth it to take the time to devise the opening of the story and make brief notes, which will make writing the story easier.

Writing a Story ★

Write your story using the notes you made on the opposite page. Write the title and the author's name—that's you! Then draw a picture. Write in neat cursive handwriting. You'll probably need to finish your story on extra pieces of paper.

Title:

By:

Answers may vary

Remind your child that carefully planned written notes are very helpful in writing the final version of a story. Explain that a useful middle stage in writing a story is a draft or rough version that can be revised. Provide scrap paper for this activity.

Write this funny poem in your best cursive handwriting.
Remember: Write the title of the poem first.

The Young Lady of Niger

There was a young lady of Niger
Who smiled as she rode on a tiger.
They returned from the ride
With the lady inside,
And a smile on the face of the tiger!

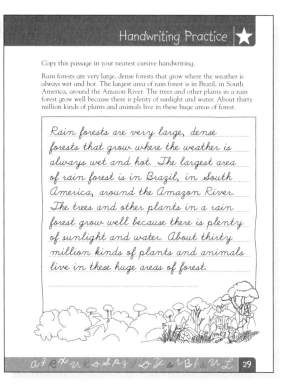

The Young Lady of Niger

There was a young lady of Niger
Who smiled as she rode on a tiger.
They returned from the ride
With the lady inside,
And a smile on the face of the tiger!

Write about the poem. Say if you like it or not, and give your reasons.

Answers may vary

Your child should always take pride in presenting all written work as neatly as possible. You might like to ask your child to write and illustrate a favorite poem or a few sentences from a story.

Copy this passage in your neatest cursive handwriting.

Rain forests are very large, dense forests that grow where the weather is always wet and hot. The largest area of rain forest is in Brazil, in South America, around the Amazon River. The trees and other plants in a rain forest grow well because there is plenty of sunlight and water. About thirty million kinds of plants and animals live in these huge areas of forest.

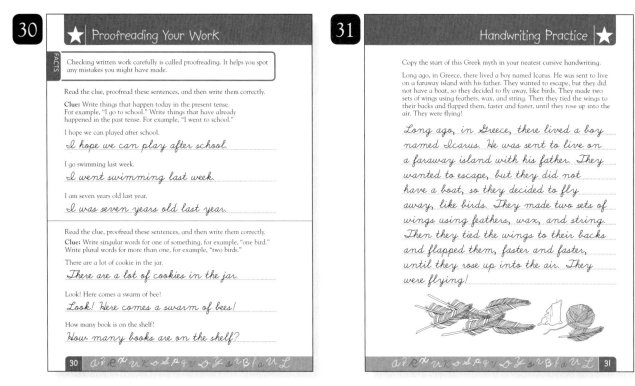

Rain forests are very large, dense forests that grow where the weather is always wet and hot. The largest area of rain forest is in Brazil, in South America, around the Amazon River. The trees and other plants in a rain forest grow well because there is plenty of sunlight and water. About thirty million kinds of plants and animals live in these huge areas of forest.

Remember, regular practice will improve your child's handwriting. Provide passages from magazines or newspapers for copying. Explain that neat handwriting is an essential communication tool.

FACTS
Checking written work carefully is called proofreading. It helps you spot any mistakes you might have made.

Read the clue, proofread these sentences, and then write them correctly.

Clue: Write things that happen today in the present tense. For example, "I go to school." Write things that have already happened in the past tense. For example, "I went to school."

I hope we can played after school.
I hope we can play after school.

I go swimming last week.
I went swimming last week.

I am seven years old last year.
I was seven years old last year.

Read the clue, proofread these sentences, and then write them correctly.

Clue: Write singular words for one of something, for example, "one bird." Write plural words for more than one, for example, "two birds."

There are a lot of cookie in the jar.
There are a lot of cookies in the jar.

Look! Here comes a swarm of bee!
Look! Here comes a swarm of bees!

How many book is on the shelf?
How many books are on the shelf?

Your child should understand and use the terms "present tense," "past tense," "singular," and "plural" with confidence. It is a valuable skill to be able to recognize and correct errors in written work.

Copy the start of this Greek myth in your neatest cursive handwriting.

Long ago, in Greece, there lived a boy named Icarus. He was sent to live on a faraway island with his father. They wanted to escape, but they did not have a boat, so they decided to fly away, like birds. They made two sets of wings using feathers, wax, and string. Then they tied the wings to their backs and flapped them, faster and faster, until they rose up into the air. They were flying!

Long ago, in Greece, there lived a boy named Icarus. He was sent to live on a faraway island with his father. They wanted to escape, but they did not have a boat, so they decided to fly away, like birds. They made two sets of wings using feathers, wax, and string. Then they tied the wings to their backs and flapped them, faster and faster, until they rose up into the air. They were flying!

Advise your child to read through a piece of text before copying it as handwriting practice. Allow about five to 10 minutes for this activity, depending upon your child's writing speed.

★ Writing Sentences

Write the sentences below in cursive handwriting. Write each sentence twice, then put a check (✓) against the one you think is neater. **Remember:** Use punctuation marks and put uppercase letters in the correct places.

i wonder when the rain will stop

I wonder when the rain will stop.

I wonder when the rain will stop.

james turned when I called his name

James turned when I called his name.

James turned when I called his name.

wow what a great sports car

Wow! What a great sports car.

Wow! What a great sports car.

Now write four sentences of your own using words from the box.

uncle	rain	goes	train

Answers may vary

Check that your child uses the correct punctuation marks when writing sentences on this page. Remember, independent writing is not easy. Praise the effort to help build confidence.

Handwriting Practice ★

Write this passage in your neatest cursive handwriting.

Dolphins are part of the same animal family as whales. They live in oceans and rivers in groups called pods. They are very smart animals and seem to like being with people. Dolphins make different noises as they play and feed together. These noises are their way of talking to each other.

Dolphins are part of the same animal family as whales. They live in oceans and rivers in groups called pods. They are very smart animals and seem to like being with people. Dolphins make different noises as they play and feed together. These noises are their way of talking to each other.

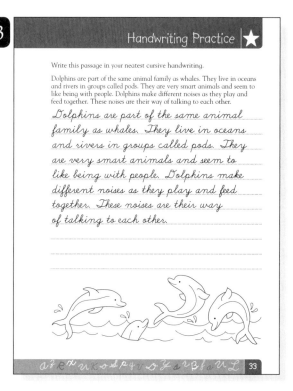

Short but regular practice will help your child achieve a fluent, legible, fast, and increasingly confident cursive handwriting style. That will help produce good written work.

★ More Proofreading

Read this passage carefully. Check for mistakes and underline any errors you find. Rewrite the passage in your neatest cursive handwriting. Use correct spellings, uppercase and lowercase letters, and punctuation marks. **Hint:** The passage contains 24 errors.

kenneth grahame

kenneth grahame was born in scotland in 1859 he had a sun whose name was alastair but he call his son mouse he told his son stories about animals that lived by a riverbank he wrote the stories down in a book the title of the book is the wind in the willows.

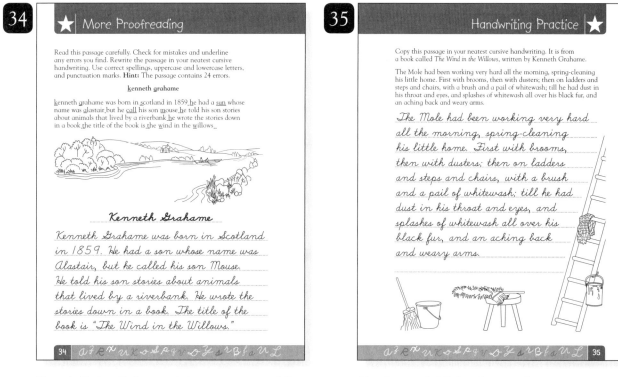

Kenneth Grahame

Kenneth Grahame was born in Scotland in 1859. He had a son whose name was Alastair, but he called his son Mouse. He told his son stories about animals that lived by a riverbank. He wrote the stories down in a book. The title of the book is "The Wind in the Willows."

Your child should first read the text very carefully, identifying and marking errors, and then rewrite it correctly. It's important to develop the habit of checking written work.

Handwriting Practice ★

Copy this passage in your neatest cursive handwriting. It is from a book called *The Wind in the Willows*, written by Kenneth Grahame.

The Mole had been working very hard all the morning, spring-cleaning his little home. First with brooms, then with dusters; then on ladders and steps and chairs, with a brush and a pail of whitewash; till he had dust in his throat and eyes, and splashes of whitewash all over his black fur, and an aching back and weary arms.

The Mole had been working very hard all the morning, spring-cleaning his little home. First with brooms, then with dusters; then on ladders and steps and chairs, with a brush and a pail of whitewash; till he had dust in his throat and eyes, and splashes of whitewash all over his black fur, and an aching back and weary arms.

Check your child's handwriting for consistent letter formation, smooth joins, and correct punctuation. Stress that it's important to read a passage carefully before copying it.

★ Planning Nonfiction

FACTS Nonfiction writing is about facts—things that are true.

Make a plan for a piece of nonfiction writing by answering the questions below. It can be about something that happened at school or information about a science topic, for example. Before writing the full piece on the opposite page, make brief notes to help you.

What is the piece of writing about?

<u>Answers may vary</u>

What is the title of your piece?

<u>Answers may vary</u>

What kind of nonfiction is it? For example, is it about an event in your life or in history, or a description of an animal?

<u>Answers may vary</u>

Are there people in the piece? <u>Answers may vary</u>

Where or when does it take place? <u>Answers may vary</u>

What interesting details will you include in your piece? For example, will you include conversations in it?

<u>Answers may vary</u>

What happens in the end? <u>Answers may vary</u>

Your child should use this page to plan a piece of nonfiction writing by jotting down short notes using single words or phrases. Explain that careful planning of written work ensures better content.

Writing Nonfiction ★

Begin by writing the title of the nonfiction piece and the author's name—that's your name! Write it in your best cursive handwriting, using the plan and notes you made on the opposite page.
Remember: Use paragraphs in your piece.

by ....

Answers may vary

Your child should refer to the plan and notes before writing the piece. Provide a separate sheet of paper for a rough draft. Remind your child to use paragraphs to split the different parts of the piece.

★ More Sentences

Write the sentences below in cursive handwriting. Write each sentence twice, then put a check (✔) against the one you think is neater. **Remember:** Use punctuation marks and put uppercase letters in the correct places.

do you like my new watch

Do you like my new watch?
Do you like my new watch?

will you show me how to skip please

Will you show me how to skip, please?
Will you show me how to skip, please?

lets go swimming tomorrow

Let's go swimming tomorrow.
Let's go swimming tomorrow.

Now write four sentences of your own using words from the box.

coin	without	know	young

Answers may vary

Encourage your child to read aloud the sentences first and then decide whether they are statements or questions. For the second activity, explain that planning the sentences will make writing easier and improve its quality.

Handwriting Practice ★

Copy this short passage about the Amazon River in cursive handwriting. Write as neatly as you can.

The Amazon River in South America is the second-longest river in the world. It flows from mountains called the Andes for almost 4,000 miles into the Atlantic Ocean on the coast of Brazil. For most of its length, the river flows through areas of very thick tropical forest called rain forest, the home of a wide variety of plant and animal life.

The Amazon River in South America is the second-longest river in the world. It flows from mountains called the Andes for almost 4,000 miles into the Atlantic Ocean on the coast of Brazil. For most of its length, the river flows through areas of very thick tropical forest called rain forest, the home of a wide variety of plant and animal life.

Ensure that your child takes ample time to write this passage and does not rush through it. Check the written work for correct spellings, neat handwriting, and equal spaces between words.

★ Planning a Letter

Imagine that someone has sent you a very special birthday gift—a new computer! Plan a thank-you letter. **Remember:** Write short, quick notes. They do not need to be written neatly.

Write these words as labels on the letter plan below.

- Your name and address
- Your signature
- Dear _____,
- Love from _____
- Your message
- The date

Make your notes here:

Dear

Answers may vary

Your name and address
The date

Your message

Love from
Your signature

Write the person's name and address on the envelope. Draw a stamp. **Remember:** Write the zip code if you know it.

Answers may vary

Discuss the conventions of letter writing and layout with your child. Help to write the labels in the correct positions. Explain the importance of writing the correct address and zip code on the envelope.

Writing a Letter ★

Look at the plan and notes you made on the opposite page before writing your thank-you letter. Write in your neatest cursive handwriting. **Remember:** Write your address, the date, and the name of the person you are writing to. Sign your name at the end.

Answers may vary

Your child should write the letter carefully, referring to the plan. Provide a separate sheet of paper for a rough draft. Children often enjoy writing their signatures.

★ Favorite Things

FACTS

Proper nouns and the main words in titles all start with uppercase letters.

Write your favorite thing for each of the topics listed below.
Write in your neatest cursive handwriting.

color
movie
food
book
sport
animal
music group
TV program

Answers may vary

Now write the name of your best friend in cursive handwriting. Then draw a picture of him or her.

Answers may vary

Make sure that your child understands the use of uppercase letters at the beginning of proper nouns. Offer a reminder to use lowercase letters when naming a favorite color or food.

Handwriting Practice ★

Copy this passage in your neatest cursive handwriting. It is from *The Jungle Book*, by Rudyard Kipling.

It was seven o'clock of a very warm evening in the Seeonee Hills when Father Wolf woke up from his day's rest, scratched himself, yawned, and spread out his paws one after the other to get rid of the sleepy feeling in their tips. Mother Wolf lay with her big gray nose dropped across her four tumbling, squealing cubs, and the moon shone into the mouth of the cave where they all lived.

It was seven o'clock of a very warm evening in the Seeonee Hills when Father Wolf woke up from his day's rest, scratched himself, yawned, and spread out his paws one after the other to get rid of the sleepy feeling in their tips. Mother Wolf lay with her big gray nose dropped across her four tumbling, squealing cubs, and the moon shone into the mouth of the cave where they all lived.

Remind your child to read through the whole passage carefully before beginning. Offer help with difficult or unfamiliar words, if necessary. Remember to praise consistent letter formation and neat handwriting.

⭐ Planning a Book Review

FACTS Fiction writing is about people and things that are made up or not real.

Make a plan for a book review of a book you have read.
Answer the questions below and write brief notes about the book.

What is the name of the book and the author?

Answers may vary

What is the book about?

Answers may vary

Who are the main characters in the book? **Remember:** Characters are the people in the book.

Answers may vary

What are the events in the book? **Remember:** Events are the things that happen in the book.

Answers may vary

What is your opinion of the book? Give reasons for liking or disliking it. **Remember:** Your opinion is what you think of the book.

Answers may vary

Help your child to plan a book review. Stress that it's important to think carefully about the book, characters, events, and whether it was enjoyable or not. Provide extra paper for making notes, if necessary.

Writing a Book Review ⭐

Write the book review in your best cursive handwriting using the plan and notes you made on the opposite page. **Remember:** Give a title to your book review and use paragraphs to make it easier to read and understand.

Answers may vary

Writing a book review will make it easier for your child to describe characters and events as well as express personal opinions and give reasons for them. Ensure that your child refers to the plan and notes before writing the final version. Provide a separate sheet of paper for a rough draft.

⭐ A Poem

Copy this poem in your neatest cursive handwriting.

Clouds

White sheep, white sheep,
On a blue hill,
When the wind stops
You all stand still.
When the wind blows
You walk away slow.
White sheep, white sheep,
Where do you go?

Christina Rossetti

Clouds

White sheep, white sheep,
On a blue hill,
When the wind stops
You all stand still.
When the wind blows
You walk away slow.
White sheep, white sheep,
Where do you go?

Christina Rossetti

Encourage your child to copy the poem correctly and neatly. Each line should begin with an uppercase letter.

Personal Profile ⭐

Fill in your personal profile in your best cursive handwriting.
Sign your name, then write the date at the bottom.

PERSONAL PROFILE

Name
Age
Date of birth
Address

Zip code
Parents
Brothers
Sisters
Best friends
Pets
Signature
Date

Answers may vary

This page marks your child's completion of the handwriting activities in this book. Note the progress made by comparing this final page to earlier ones. Offer lots of praise.